THE ART OF SELF-DIRECTED LEARNING

23 tips for giving yourself an unconventional education

BLAKE BOLES

TELLS PEAK PRESS

Dedicated to Jim, Grace, Dev, Mom, and Dad

The Art of Self-Directed Learning

In high school or college, did you ever take a class on self-education? A class that helped you learn how to learn?

Neither did I.

Yet whenever we finish our formal schooling—and often during it—that's exactly what we need to do: learn all sorts of important things, on our own, without a blueprint.

Ask yourself, do you want to:

- build something from scratch: a website, a business, a house?
- pursue a course of self-study or personal research?
- work in a field unrelated to your degree or previous experience?

- improve yourself in a deep, meaningful way?
- travel independently?

Yes? Then you need self-directed learning. Because for these kind of challenges, no one will hold your hand. The only way to solve the problem is to learn your way there.

But self-directed learning (which I will define in the first few chapters) isn't just a collection of practical tools for getting stuff done: it's also a mindset that can help you lead a life very different from that of your friends, family, or society.

This book is a compilation of the wisdom, stories, and tools I've garnered from working with self-directed learners for more than a decade. Unlike my first two books, which I wrote specifically for teenagers and young adults facing the question of college, I created *The Art of Self-Directed Learning* for:

- high school and college students who are passionate about learning, aren't content to just "do school," and want to take more control of their educations

- teenage homeschoolers and unschoolers who want to become more effective and engaged self-educators
- young adults who aren't going to college and who are seeking guidance in their ongoing educations and career pursuits
- parents who want to support their kids (or future kids) as self-directed learners
- skeptical relatives and friends who want to see that self-directed learning isn't about mindless wandering, avoiding work, or being irresponsible
- adults of all ages who want to shape their careers to better reflect their beliefs
- anyone who never wants to stop learning

The book starts with an explanation of who I am and where I've been, and then it provides 23 stories and insights for becoming a better self-directed learner. I begin by defining self-directed learning and then discuss motivation, learning online, learning offline, meta-learning, and building a career as a self-educator. The final chapter discusses how nature, nurture, luck, and mindset influence self-directed learning. An original illustration by my friend Shona Warwick-Smith accompanies each chapter to further illuminate its ideas.

Here's a preview of the upcoming chapters:

INTRODUCTION

What I Learned at Summer Camp, Down the Rabbit Hole, Back Out Again, and What I Found

The story of my own education, how I joined the unschooling movement, and why I became a cheerleader for self-directed learning.

LEARNERS AND LEARNING

1. The Girl Who Sailed Around the World

Self-directed learning starts with a dream to go farther, see more, and become more than others tell you is possible. But dreaming alone is not enough; you must fight to turn your dreams into reality.

2. What Self-Directed Learners Do

Self-directed learners take full responsibility for their educations, careers, and lives. Think hard about where you're going, research all your options, and then move boldly forward.

3. What Self-Directed Learners Don't Do

Don't throw the baby out with the bathwater.
Open yourself to the world and soak up as much learning as possible.

4. Consensual Learning

Reject the tyranny of forced learning, no matter how desirable the end result.

MOTIVATION

LEARNING ONLINE

LEARNING OFFLINE

META-LEARNING

SELF-DIRECTED EARNING

Whether you're a veteran self-directed learner, the parent of a highly independent child, a student looking for new options, or a newcomer to self-education, this book will give you the tools and inspiration to learn more effectively and give yourself an unconventional education in a conventional world.

Ready? Let's begin.

INTRODUCTION

What
I Learned at
Summer Camp

When I was 11, I went away to summer camp for the first time. I didn't brush my teeth for two weeks. It was fantastic.

The next summer, I had a camp girlfriend. She was 14. I told her I was 13. We held hands for one steamy week. Then she discovered that I was actually 12, and I learned that lying to make someone like you doesn't work.

A few summers later, I joined the camp's toughest backpacking trip. I helped plan the route, pack the food, and lead the group. We hiked to a high-elevation river, played on natural water slides, and ate orange drink-mix powder straight from the bag. Life was good.

Blake (left), age 15, eating orange drink-mix powder on a backpacking trip

Then, as I did every August, I went back to school, and life seemed to lose its color.

I did well in school. But that didn't make things better, because camp and school felt like two totally different worlds:

- At camp, I had control over my schedule. At school, it was predetermined.
- At camp, I could go deep into my interests. At school, I could only skim the surface.
- At camp, I was a social freelancer. At school, group identity meant everything.
- At camp, adults treated me like a person. At school, they treated me like my test score.
- At camp, I went because I chose to. At school, I went because I had to.

School taught me how to memorize a fact until Friday and alter the margins on an essay to create a higher page count; camp taught me how to figure out what I want, take the initiative, conquer my fears, own my victories, and learn from my failures.

To my teenage sensibilities, the annual ratio of camp to school didn't make sense. Why didn't I go to camp most of the year and then head off to school for a couple months to learn grammar, algebra, and whatever else camp didn't teach?

Down the Rabbit Hole

My quiet frustration with school didn't find an outlet until halfway through college when, by a stroke of luck, a friend handed me a book by New York City public schoolteacher John Taylor Gatto.

12 Action Themes of John Gatto's Guerrilla Curriculum

(A cost-free method to restore primary experience and intellectual quality to schools)

(1) Substantial community service
(2) Apprenticeships
(3) Parent partnerships (on school time)
(4) Team Projects (gardens, cross-age tutoring, talent shows, food co-ops, etc.)
(5) Independent study
(6) Work/Study (including starting a business)
(7) Mentorships
(8) Solitudes (fishing, hiking, contemplation, silence, etc.)
(9) Adventures/Discoveries (mapping, exploration, meandering, challenge, etc.)
(10) Field Curriculum (furnishing an apartment, shadowing an employee at the jobsite, analyzing the characteristics of good and bad swimming pools, etc.)
(11) Improvisational Play in Groups without Guidance
(12) Flex-time; flex-space; flex-sequencing; flex text selection

Sparkle and Shine in the Face of Darkness

Excerpt from a handout provided by John Taylor Gatto

Gatto taught for 30 years in some of the best and worst schools in Manhattan. He won multiple awards for his "guerrilla curriculum" of hands-on and community-based activities. Then he quit teaching because he didn't want to "hurt kids to make a living" anymore, and he started writing—and speaking across the globe—about alternatives to traditional school.

Suddenly a switch flipped. Gatto's guerrilla curriculum and devastating critiques joined forces with my quiet frustration with school. Together they staged a coup in my mind and conspired to take my life in a whole new direction.

Within a month I had abandoned my old college major and custom-designed a new one that let me study education theory full-time. I gave up my dream of becoming a research scientist in order to spend time at tiny experimental schools, read every book I could find about educational alternatives, and organize a class for fellow undergraduates called *Never Taught to Learn*. My mind was on fire. Little did I know then that within the next five years, my experiences would lead me to my own self-directed career path.

Leading the Unschool Adventures South America group, 2011

After graduating in 2004, I returned to work at my childhood wilderness summer camp and also got involved with a new one, Not Back to School Camp: the camp for teenage unschoolers (homeschoolers who don't follow a traditional curriculum in favor of a more self-directed approach).

The campers at Not Back to School Camp—some of whom dropped out of high school, and many of whom never went to school in the first place—were mature, self-knowledgeable, and passionate. They communicated clearly, actively questioned the world around them, and considered their dreams and goals carefully. They were, I realized, exactly who I wanted to work with. Within a few years I decided to build my career around hanging out with young-adult unschoolers, full-time, by creating my little travel and education company, Unschool Adventures.

Soon I was working at two summer camps and running my own leadership programs, writing retreats, and international trips every year, fulfilling my childhood dream of doing camp-style adventures year-round. I thought I'd found the promised land, but something kept nagging at me.

. . . And Back Out Again

As I went deeper into unschooling, I realized I was riding into the Wild-Wild-West of alternative education. Unschooling was an open and leaderless movement, and like any such movement, both the best and worst rose quickly to the surface.

In its best moments, the philosophy of unschooling promoted listening deeply to one's child, treating her as a person worthy of adult-level respect, and providing a wide variety of educational options. If her choice included school or college, so be it. In this worldview, everything (including structured learning) was an experiment from which to be learned.

In its worst moments, unschooling vilified the entire world of school, structure, teachers, teaching, and classes, labeling any sort of formal education as fundamentally coercive.

The first vision of unschooling spoke truth to me but the second didn't. My own summer camp and college experiences involved plenty of teaching, classes, and structure from which I, and others like me, sincerely benefited.

Unfortunately, the second vision of unschooling had semantics on its side. Because what was un-schooling if not something against school? This proved a difficult trap to escape, and in promoting unschooling, I, too, found myself bashing school.

That's when I decided that I needed to find a positive vision of what I believed. So I began searching across the United States and the wider world to discover the roots of what I loved about unschooling, summer camps, world travel, entrepreneurship, and certain schools and colleges.

What I Found

By 2009, I had poked my head into some wildly different places, from the tango halls of Buenos Aires to Stanford University's Design School. On my journey, I interviewed dropouts and Ivy Leaguers, bankers and artists, punks and programmers, off-the-grid hippies and tech-obsessed "edupreneurs." I met an endless number of incredibly thoughtful and caring parents from across the philosophical and political spectrum. And I reflected deeply on my own education, both formal and informal.

As I conducted my research, a pattern emerged. Pretty much everyone, it seemed, wanted to help young people do the same things:

- solve their own problems
- become their own teachers
- work on interesting problems
- collaborate and connect with others
- be leaders in their own lives

Teachers wanted this, unschoolers wanted this, parents wanted this, and young people themselves wanted this. They all agreed that these skills would serve them both personally and professionally. The only problem? No one agreed on what to call this package.

But to me, one term was a clear winner: *self-directed learning.* It was a positive term that symbolizes freedom, choice, and embracing learning wherever you may find it. It was the perfect term for independent learning in the twenty-first century, and it needed another cheerleader.

What you hold in your hands now contains the best adventures, insights, lessons, and stories that I've gathered on my journey of discovery. This book is also a love letter to self-directed learners everywhere: the unschoolers, independent learners inside school, summer campers, adventurers, entrepreneurs, parents, and travelers who continually inspire me to keep working on this funky frontier in the world of education.

If you like what you read, and especially if you have a story to share, I hope you'll drop me a line: yourstruly@blakeboles.com.

Photo courtesy of Blake Club, my anonymous online fan club (most likely composed of campers and students with whom I've worked) that photoshops my head onto photographs in weird, hilarious, and often disturbing ways (https://www.facebook.com/BlakeClub)

LEARNERS
AND
LEARNING

1

The Girl Who Sailed Around the World

Want to know what self-directed learning looks like? Look no further than Laura Dekker, who in 2009 announced her plan to sail around the world by herself.

That's impressive in itself, but the most interesting part: she was only 14.

Laura, a Dutch citizen, was aiming to become the youngest person to solo circumnavigate the globe—and she was prepared. Laura was born on a boat, spent the first four years of her life at sea, started solo-sailing at age six, began competitive racing at age seven, solo-sailed from the Netherlands to England at age 13, and had outfitted her vessel specifically for round-the-world travel. Her parents fully supported her decision and trusted her capacity to safely make the journey.

But when Laura revealed her plan to the world, the Dutch child welfare court took legal action to prevent her from undertaking what they considered an obviously irresponsible adventure.

Beyond their safety concerns, the court argued that, by missing a year of high school, Laura would fall dangerously behind in her education.

•   •   •

Would Laura be ready for the challenge of sailing around the world? Would she learn as much or more from sailing around the world than from sitting in high school? Was this a dream she could defer to the future without losing an important part of who she was?

Laura knew the answers to these questions. Her parents knew the answers. But the Dutch child welfare authorities didn't know.

In moments like these, we face a choice: do we give in to an authority that claims to know what's best for us, or do we stand up for what we believe is right and important?

Laura could have accepted the court's pronouncement. She could have abandoned her dream. She could have told herself that, despite possessing the attitude, skills, and preparations necessary to run her own life, she would let someone else run it for her.

But that's not what self-directed learners do, and that's not what Laura did.

•   •   •

Soliciting support from an international community of parents, sailors, and educators, Laura and her family fought the court's decision.

The battle wasn't easy. At one point, the state made Laura a ward of the court, which she protested by running away to the Caribbean island of St. Martin.

Eight court cases and a full year later, a second Dutch court overruled the first, and two weeks later, Laura sailed away from Gibraltar in her 38-foot yacht named Guppy. She circled the world in a year and half, finishing at age 16, the youngest girl to ever sail around the world by herself.

Self-directed learning starts with a dream to go farther, see more, and become more than others tell you is possible. But dreaming alone is not enough; you must fight to turn your dreams into reality.

2

What Self-Directed Learners Do

O f course, you don't need to sail around the world, wage legal battles, or do anything as grandiose to be a self-directed learner. In more than a decade of research and travel, I've met very few "brilliant" or "highly gifted" self-learners, but I have met innumerable people who have simply decided to take full responsibility for their learning. "Genius," as John Taylor Gatto says, "is as common as dirt."

Self-directed learners are normal people who wake up in the morning, put on their clothes, and eat their breakfasts. They brush their teeth, check their computers, and feed their pets. Then they ask themselves: Where do I want to go in life, and how will I get myself there?

When self-directed learners choose to go to school, they arrive on time, take notes, and do their homework—because school is taking them where they want to go.

When self-directed learners choose to go to work, they put in long hours, volunteer for the hard tasks that other people avoid, and get promoted—because work is taking them where they want to go.

The difference between self-directed learners and everyone else is: As soon as school or work stops serving their life goals, they don't stick around. They ditch the well-trodden path, bust out the map and compass, and cut cross-country to virgin territory.

Instead of putting up with a miserable or unproductive school situation, a self-directed learner figures out how to get an education on his own terms. He changes his approach to school, finds a different school, or leaves school altogether.

If work becomes unfulfilling or no longer serves a self-directed learner's purpose, instead of resigning herself to a life of frustrating or meaningless employment, she takes clear steps to better her situation. She negotiates different workplace responsibilities, interviews for a better job, or starts her own business.

Self-directed learners take full responsibility for their educations, careers, and lives. Think hard about where you're going, research all your options, and then move boldly forward.

3

What
Self-Directed
Learners
Don't Do

Back in college I led a course for other undergraduates called *Never Taught to Learn*, a crash-course introduction to alternative education theory.

At the end of the semester, one of my students gave me a knitted wool beanie as a gift.

On one side, it read:

Teach Yourself to Learn

and on the other:

Learn to Teach Yourself

As you rotated the beanie, the phrases joined together to form a never-ending sentence: *Teach Yourself to Learn to Teach Yourself to Learn to. . . .*

I lost that beanie only days later in a behemoth grocery store called Berkeley Bowl, but its words stuck with me like a mantra, reminding me that teaching and learning are two sides of the same coin.

Self-directed learners can be defined as much by what they do as by what they don't. One thing they don't do is universally condemn teachers, structure, or formal instruction. They recognize that such methods, when freely elected, have their place.

Here are a few more things that self-directed learners don't do:

- Self-directed learners don't spend much time in places where they are constantly bored and unengaged.
- Self-directed learners don't hide their passions and interests in order to please others.

- Self-directed learners don't give up on their goals at the first setback.
- Self-directed learners don't mope when they find themselves in an uncomfortable or foreign situation; they approach life as an anthropologist does, learning whatever they can.
- Self-directed learners don't assume they can (or should) learn everything on their own.
- Self-directed learners don't worry that if they don't learn something right now, it will be too late. They know they can always find a way.

Don't throw the baby out with the bathwater. Open yourself to the world and soak up as much learning as possible.

4

Consensual Learning

Directly after college I took an Emergency Medical Technician course. Hungry to build practical, hands-on skills after 16 years of abstract academia, I hoped the first class would jump straight into the good stuff: how to stop massive arterial bleeding, stick a pen into someone's trachea to help them breathe again, or splint a femur fracture.

Instead, we talked about consent.

Emergency Medical Technicians, I learned, can make all sorts of mistakes. Show up at a car crash and just start moving people around, and you might aggravate a spine injury. Treat a child without her parent's permission, and you might get yourself in deep trouble.

The basic principle was: Don't help someone without asking first. Get consent first. Because when you think you're helping, you might actually be hurting.

After that lesson, I thought back to my entire K–12 schooling experience. Despite the number of kind-hearted and well-intentioned people who played a part in it, how many ever asked for my consent? How many asked me (and seriously engaged me in) the questions: Did I actually want to go to school? Did I actually think this assignment was a good idea? Was this class actually worth my time? And what else might I have done with my time instead of sitting bored?

School, I realized, is a terrible place to learn consent—which is a shame, considering that consent is the cornerstone of every healthy relationship and community I've ever encountered.

To me, consent means:

- understanding what you're committing to
- knowing what the alternatives are
- saying "yes" while retaining the power to say "no"

To illustrate, let's say you're thinking about signing up for a cooking class. Consenting fully to this class means reading the course description carefully, finding reviews of the class, comparing it with other available classes, and understanding the refund policy.

Having done this research, you're ready to make an informed decision about taking the cooking class, while always reserving the power to walk out.

Now imagine applying this method to every educational situation in your life. That's the daily work of a self-directed learner.

A self-directed high school graduate doesn't simply enroll in the "best college" available to her. She tours campuses, interviews professors, chats with current students, and tracks down recent graduates. She considers multiple colleges. She considers not going to college at all. And if she enrolls, she forever remembers that she can change schools or leave college altogether, if necessary.

A self-directed teenage homeschooler doesn't assume that his parents' choices will automatically make him successful. As soon as possible, he begins taking control of his own education. He uses books, the Internet, and other people to research and inform his decisions. If his parents' curriculum no longer feels meaningful, he advocates for his own interests. If he wants to try school, he proposes it as an experiment. He sees himself as an active participant, not a passive pawn, in his own education.

A self-directed parent who wants her kid to take violin lessons doesn't just sign him up for lessons. She explains her reasoning to him: "I want you to appreciate music," for example. She suggests other activities that could provide the same benefits, such as guitar lessons, digital composing, or attending the symphony. She sets clear expectations for any classes or tutoring: "I want you to give your best effort to three lessons." She gives him the space to think, weigh his options, and respond. She doesn't force, cajole, or emotionally blackmail. She treats her child as the budding adult that he will soon become, and when he says "no," that means no. And when she gets antsy, she signs up for violin lessons herself and leads by example.

C.S. Lewis wrote, "Of all tyrannies, a tyranny sincerely exercised for the good of its victims may be the most oppressive." Education is no exception. To become a self-directed learner is to become, in the words of my friend Ethan Mitchell, a consensual learner.

Reject the tyranny of forced learning, no matter how desirable the end result.

Don't you make your children learn anything?

Make? No. I don't make them learn anything. I inquire. I suggest. I offer incentives. But I do not make. I am not their central planner. That job is taken. My job isn't to decree what they will be good at or what they will do or how they will do it. I am not king in their lives. They are sovereign. Their minds belong to them. It is their property, after all.

My job is to approach them with humility and know that my ability to discern what they are to be or to do or to excel in is nothing compared to theirs. My job is to assist them in their discernment. To make experiences, work, play, resources, teachers, mentors, and collaborators available to them to help them as they construct themselves. To talk things through with them, but not talk it all to death. My job is to sit down, shut up, and serve when I can. I direct nothing. Less of me. More of them.

—Ana Martin

("The Libertarian Homeschooler" on Facebook)

MOTIVATION

5

Autonomy, Mastery, Purpose

Fourteen-year-old Celina Dill of Whidbey Island, Washington, was a straight-A but burnt-out public school student until her dad suggested that they explore other educational options. Many conversations later, Celina, her older sister, and her dad decided together to move out of their rented house, store their possessions in a friend's barn, and travel on a shoestring budget across Europe for six months. Teaching dance classes, eating frugally, and staying with 50 different families in 17 different countries along the way, the family traveled the continent for less money that it would have cost to continue renting their home back on Whidbey Island.

When she returned to the United States, Celina went back to school but couldn't shake the feeling that something had changed deep within her. Halfway through her freshman year of high school, she began going half-time. Then she transitioned to online school.

"I quickly realized," Celina later told me at Not Back to School Camp, "that there was a lot I wanted to do with my life that I simply couldn't do in school." So she ultimately decided to stop going to school altogether.

Celina dedicated her newfound free time to cooking, weight lifting, teaching dance classes, doing portrait photography, playing the harp, writing, and exploring her local area. Her dad, a dance teacher, artist, and industrial designer—and an art college dropout himself—supported Celina's choice to self-direct her learning. Her mom (who was divorced from her father) was very resistant at first, but with consistent advocacy by Celina and her sister, eventually came around.

By 16, Celina was very independent and wanted a home of her own, so she began researching low-cost alternative housing. She learned that she could build a small house on a wheeled trailer frame that would give her the personal space she craved at a very low price—if she built it herself. With the extensive support of her dad, Celina began designing and building a tiny house that she could park anywhere and call her own.

To develop the necessary construction and design skills, Celina began by apprenticing with a local architect for nine months. During that time she connected with local builders, collected scrap materials around town, and rebuilt a mobile home chassis with the help of a welding instructor. To earn the money for materials, she taught dance, took portraits, built websites, and took a data entry job.

Today, at age 19, Celina is installing the floors and fixtures on her tiny house. She's parking it on a friend's property where she pays $400 a month for land, water, power, and garden space. She's happy, engaged with meaningful work, and has a bright outlook on her future.

•   •   •

Celina's story is inspiring and intimidating at the same time because it's easy to read about people like her and tell yourself, "She's self-motivated; I'm not."

But highly motivated self-directed learners like Celina don't simply rise from the primordial ooze. There are three consistent ingredients in stories like hers:

- autonomy
- mastery
- purpose

Every self-directed learner requires a large degree of autonomy: freedom to make his or her own decisions. Celina obtained her autonomy by taking time away from school to travel the world and then choosing to become a full-time self-educator with the (eventual) support of both parents.

Next, self-directed learners require mastery: the opportunity to get really good at various skills instead of only skimming the surface. Celina pursued mastery as a dance teacher, photographer, musician, and tiny house builder: each a big challenge with lots of room for improvement.

Finally, self-directed learners need a sense of purpose: the feeling that their pursuits are connected to a greater mission. For Celina, building her tiny house (and earning the money to fund it) was connected to the greater desire to achieve independence, create her own world, and have a meaningful relationship to everything around her.

The secret sauce of self-directed learning isn't much of a secret at all: find your autonomy, mastery, and purpose, and you'll find your way.

Autotelic: another term for "self-directed learner"

au·to·te·lic: having a purpose in and not apart from itself

An autotelic person needs few material possessions and little entertainment, comfort, power, or fame because so much of what he or she does is already rewarding. Because such persons experience flow in work, in family life, when interacting with people, when eating, even when alone with nothing to do, they are less dependent on the external rewards that keep others motivated to go on with a life composed of routines. They are more autonomous and independent because they cannot be as easily manipulated with threats or rewards from the outside. At the same time, they are more involved with everything around them because they are fully immersed in the current of life.

—Mihaly Csikszentmihalyi

Author of *Flow: The Psychology of Optimal Experience*

6

Discipline,
Dissected

T he writer John Cheever put on his suit every morning and rode the elevator down in his apartment building.

Instead of exiting at the ground floor, he continued to a storage room in the basement.

There, he shed his clothes and wrote in his underwear until noon. Then he dressed again, took the elevator back up for lunch, and continued his day, having completed his most important work.

The first and most rational fear of a self-directed learner is, *How will I get things done?* If Cheever is any example, then the answer is simple: Treat your life like an incredibly well-paid job. Show up every day, put in the hours, push forward, and then the magic starts to happen.

The author Stephen Pressfield calls this approach "turning professional." The idea is that we get things done by throwing away our excuses, demolishing all distractions, cutting the crap, and summoning every ounce of our self-discipline.

But we must tread carefully around the word *discipline*. As the essayist Paul Graham explains, "One of the most dangerous illusions [we] get from school is the idea that doing great things requires a lot of discipline." Many top achievers and highly creative people, Graham argues, are actually terrible procrastinators who have little discipline for tasks that bore them.

So we have two approaches to discipline. The first is putting your nose to the grindstone, shedding all distractions, and doing the work, no matter what. The second is not forcing anything, seeing procrastination as feedback, and waiting until inspiration strikes.

Both are correct.

Try this. The next time you're facing a daunting self-directed learning task—something that no one is going to make happen but you—ask yourself three questions:

- If I don't do this work, will I feel badly afterwards, perhaps even physically ill?
- When I've done this work in the past, did I feel like it made an important difference either in my life or in the world?
- When I've done this work in the past, did I just need to get over the initial hump, and then self-motivation took over?

If your answer is "yes" to all three questions, then your calling is true. It's time to disable the Wi-Fi, write in your underwear, or do whatever else is necessary to buckle down and focus.

If the answer is "no" to many of the questions, perhaps you're working on the wrong project, or you're approaching it the wrong way. Buckling down might not help here—it's time to change direction.

And if the answer to the questions is, "I don't know," or, "I don't have enough information," then it's time do a little research. Try the focused approach and watch yourself carefully. Are you feeling engaged? Is this worth your time? Then, after a period of genuine effort, ask yourself the three questions again.

For myself, I think about running and writing. If I put off a long run or a writing project for too long:

- I start to feel badly, sometimes even physically ill.
- I stop feeling like I'm making a positive difference in the world and in my health.
- I realize that I'm just avoiding the startup hump—the putting on of the shoes or the opening of the word processor—and not the work itself, which I thoroughly enjoy after I've begun.

More than anything else, the art of self-directed learning is the art of knowing what engages you, what distracts you, and what's most important to achieve in your life right now.

Gathering such knowledge requires a seemingly endless amount of reflection, discussion, and self-examination. But the payoff to this work, in the words of my friend Dev Carey, is that "discipline becomes simply remembering."

Self-discipline isn't some universal attribute that you either have or don't. It's a product of matching your actions to the work that's most important in your life.

7

Cages and Keys

I CAN'T   I COULD IF I

My first year at summer camp, I heard rumors about the Saturday evening campfire. Something strange happened afterwards, I'd heard, but no one would give me the details.

At dusk on that first Saturday, I congregated with the rest of the camp for the quarter-mile hike to the campfire site. No flashlights were allowed, and the instructors advised us to look behind as we walked through the woods. Anticipation mounted.

At 10:30 PM, as the evening's talent show ended and the bonfire coals flickered into darkness, I finally learned the Great Secret. Each of the first-time campers was going to walk back to camp, through the wilderness, in the pitch black, alone. I quaked in my poorly tied boots.

Blake, age 11, at Deer Crossing Camp with camp director Jim Wiltens

Years later, as a returning camper and instructor, I would come to relish the memory of my first "night walk," a rite of passage that no one tells you about until it's upon you.

But at that moment, as I waited for my turn to descend the ominous granite shelf, my mind erupted with fear, anxiety, and the litigious thoughts of an entitled 11-year-old. *This is ridiculous! Who do they think they are? I'll sue everyone!*

A hand fell on my shoulder. "Don't freak out," an instructor gently advised me. "We've been preparing you for this."

She was, I realized, correct.

Deer Crossing Camp was a strange and special place to grow up each summer, and not just because they asked 11-year-olds to walk through the woods alone. The very first thing you learned at Deer Crossing was that at this camp, you're not allowed to say "I can't." Not during classes, not during meals, and not even during casual conversation.

Sure, I remember thinking when I heard the rule on the first day, *like that's going to happen*. It sounded like the type of grand pronouncement that a school principal would blurt on the first day of school and never really enforce.

But then I arrived at camp and saw that everyone actually took this rule seriously.

The rule wasn't universally followed, of course, and the most serious consequence for saying "I can't" was the jeers of your fellow campers crooning in unison, "You whaaaat?"

But this strange policy completely succeeded in one respect. At Deer Crossing, you learned that every time you said "I can't," you were making a choice. Because instead of saying "I can't," the instructors gently reminded time and time again, we could say a different phrase: "I could if I."

My first "I could if I" moment was in kayaking class when we practiced flipping our boats over and escaping from them into the water. (These were whitewater-style closed-top kayaks, not open-top ones.)

During one of my flips my foot became stuck, forcing me to swallow a mouthful of water, panic, and get mad. "I can't do this stupid kayaking!" I protested. I was prepared to walk away right there, but my instructor convinced me to ask myself "I could if I" first.

What had caused my foot to stick in the kayak, and what could I do differently next time? I reluctantly began brainstorming.

> *"I could get my foot out if I . . . wore smaller shoes."*
> *"Yes, that's one option," the instructor replied. "What's another?"*
> *"If I bent forward more?"*
> *"Okay. How about one more?"*
> *I racked my brain. "If I . . . took a deeper breath to give myself more time?"*
> *"Great. Let's try that one."*

Lo and behold, on the next flip, I exited the kayak like a slippery fish.

•   •   •

If someone had introduced the "I could if I" strategy to me as an adult, I may have written it off as self-help hogwash. But to my 11-year-old self, facing the prospect of a terrifying night walk, "I could if I" was the key that unlocked my cage of self-doubt.

As my knees quivered in that cold mountain night, I took a deep breath, recomposed myself, and asked myself, "I could do this walk if I . . .

> *walked down to the edge of the granite shelf, where the dirt begins . . .*
> *walked between the two tall trees . . .*
> *and followed the rocky gully down to the forest trail.*

I took the first step. Five minutes later, I was back at camp.

Summer camp taught me that my habit of saying "I can't" was a cage, and this cage had a key called "I could if I." To escape the cage, all I had to do was pick up the key and think a little differently.

Attitude is a self-directed learner's most precious resource. For every cage, you can find a key.

Cage	Key
I can't	I could if I
I should	I choose to
I don't know	I'll find out
I wish	I'll make a plan
I hate	I prefer
I have to	I get to

8

Second Right Answers

Sean Aiken attended a standard high school in Canada, went straight into a standard public college, and graduated with a standard bachelor's degree in business.

Unfortunately, taking the standard route left Sean with no idea what to do with his life, and he possessed no method by which to figure it out.

After college everybody told Sean to "find his passion," which just frustrated him because no one ever explained exactly how to go about it. He traveled briefly, felt stumped, and moved back in with his parents.

At this point, Sean could have abandoned his pursuit of

meaningful work. He could have just taken any old job. Instead, he decided to take 52 jobs.

Coming from 16 unbroken years of formal education, Sean realized that he simply didn't know what kind of work was available to him, and therefore he couldn't make an informed career decision. So in order to figure out his options, he hatched a plan to take one new job each week for a year.

He began with his personal network, asking family and friends to let him take part in their jobs for one week at a time. As he worked, Sean wrote about his experiences on his newly registered website, OneWeekJob.com.

The story of Sean's challenge quickly spread online, and he started receiving unsolicited job offers from across North America to become a dairy farmer, advertising executive, bungee jumping instructor, baker, firefighter, and stock trader.

By the end of his journey, Sean had become a minor celebrity and decided to harness his moment of fame by writing a book, helping produce a documentary, and speaking to student groups around the world about his One Week Job project.

Sean had found his dream job—at least for the time being—and all it took was 52 little experiments.

Whether you're looking for a new career, considering college majors, or pondering your next self-directed learning project, don't just go with the first "right answer." Come up with a second, third, fourth answer—or a fifty-second. By investing the time necessary to deeply explore your options, you'll feel more motivated to follow through on your commitment.

Generate an excess of solutions for the big challenges in life, and the right answer will present itself.

LEARNING ONLINE

9

Googling Everything

START HERE

My friends and I have a running joke. Whenever one of us wonders aloud about a simple fact—how many people live in a certain city, for example—someone else responds, "If only there were some vast, free information network that we could consult. . . ."

The joke, of course, is that any of us can whip out an Internet-connected device and answer the question in seconds.

Today, looking up information online is so ridiculously easy that there's a website designed specifically to poke fun at those who neglect to do it: Let Me Google That For You (lmgtfy.com).

To have a little fun the next time your friend asks a dumb (i.e., easily searchable) question, go to the LMGTFY website, enter the search term that will answer your friend's question, and then give him the link that LMGTFY generates.

When he clicks it, a new Google window will open. The mouse cursor will move to the search box, type in the search term, and then click the submit button.

As the results load, a small box appears that says: *Was that so hard?*

LMGTFY is a snarky reminder that as information technology empowers us, it also demands that we become more self-sufficient.

As a self-directed learner, you should start with the Internet whenever you have a question you want answered. As the author Austin Kleon instructs, "Google everything. I mean everything. Google your dreams, Google your problems. Don't ask a question before you Google it."

But online learning isn't only about finding basic information; it's about harnessing the full power of the Internet to do everything in your life more effectively. Consider this story about my old college roommate, Bryan, who saved $30,000 with his smartphone.

A few years ago, Bryan broke his ankle while playing on a rope swing in Northern California. After the accident, a friend took him to the nearest hospital in San Francisco, but because Bryan didn't have health insurance, the surgery bill was going to be massive.

Lying in the hospital bed, Bryan wondered whether he was making a mistake by getting treated in California. He pulled out his smartphone and researched the cost of surgery in other parts of the United States. The state of New York, it turned out, had significantly lower costs for the specific treatment he needed. So Bryan made a few calls, secured himself admission to a new hospital, and then booked a flight that evening—all from his smartphone—saving more than $30,000 in the process.

If Bryan could do all this from his hospital bed, consider what you could accomplish by searching the Internet more effectively.

Ask yourself, can you use the Internet to:

- prepare for a job interview by studying the website, blog posts, and social media accounts of company employees and executives?
- give yourself a basic introduction to any fact, current event, or historical event?
- distinguish between factual (i.e., peer-reviewed or reasonably trustworthy) content and nonfactual content (e.g., opinion, hearsay, pseudoscience)?
- find the personal e-mail address of a minor celebrity?
- learn how to change an oil filter, butcher a chicken, or install a window?
- find any place of business and its hours, customer reviews, and driving directions?
- read three distinctly different perspectives on the same piece of news?
- figure out the cheapest way to buy a flight, book, or any other consumer product?
- use operators like quotation marks, the minus sign, and "site:" to more effectively search the web?

Each of these skills is within your power, if only you take the time to train yourself.

Not sure where to start? Just google it.

The Internet is the most powerful learning tool ever created. Use it early and often.

10

E-mailing Strangers

NEW MESSAGE

TO: SOMEONE AWESOME

FROM: ME

SUBJECT: I LOVE WHAT YOU DO

Fifteen year-old Jonah Meyer picked up a popular science book one day—a whirlwind overview of modern research—and became deeply interested in chemistry.

To sate his curiosity, Jonah began reading more science books and watching free online lectures about chemistry. He even started working through a high school chemistry textbook, but it left him wanting more. He kept searching and soon found something that looked perfect, a freshman Introduction to Chemistry course at the nearby University of Massachusetts at Amherst.

Being only 15, Jonah knew that it would be difficult (if not impossible) to enroll as an official student. So instead, he googled the professor's name, found the professor's e-mail address, and wrote an e-mail that essentially read, "Hi, my name is Jonah. I'm 15; I'm really interested in chemistry, and I'd like to sit in on your class. Would that be okay?"

The professor was delighted to hear from a student who was passionate about chemistry—and not because it was required—and told Jonah to come by on the first day of class.

Jonah and the professor worked out a deal, and over the course of the semester, Jonah attended every lecture, did every homework assignment, took every test, and passed the course. The professor couldn't offer him official course credit, but he did write him a letter of recommendation, enabling him to skip Introduction to Chemistry if he decided to later enroll at the University of Massachusetts.

My favorite part of the story is that Jonah is a middle-school dropout. The chemistry class was the first time that he had set foot in a classroom in three years. Yet he created an incredibly powerful learning experience for himself by boldly e-mailing a stranger.

If you can google someone today, there's a good chance you can find his e-mail address, too. Then, with only a minor investment of time and creativity, you can write a brief note like Jonah did. Follow these basic principles to give your first e-mail the best chance of success:

1. Keep it short. 4–6 sentences is a good length for an introductory e-mail.
2. Format for clarity. Break larger paragraphs into chunks of 1–2 sentences, and use a little bit of bolding and/or italics to highlight the most important parts.
3. Make a clear, reasonable request. Do you want this person to read something and give you feedback? Attend an event? Give you information? Introduce you to somebody else? Be straightforward and specific, avoid ambiguous requests like "please help me" or "I'd like to pick your brain," and minimize the time requirement for the other person.
4. Prove that you're serious. In other words, show the person that he won't waste his time on you. Briefly share your credibility indicators (e.g., previous experience, formal

education) and the story behind your request. And always ask someone else to proofread your e-mail before you hit *Send*.

Asking for help via e-mail is a low-cost and low-risk move with a potentially huge payoff. Who could you be writing today?

11

The Digital
Paper Trail

W ant to smile? Go find the *Girl Walk // All Day* video series online. Turn your speakers up, maximize the screen, and enjoy.

Anne Marsen, the lead dancer in *Girl Walk // All Day*, grew up as competitive dancer in New Jersey, performing in *The Nutcracker* and vying to become the best ballerina in ballet school.

But when Anne started college at the University of the Arts in Philadelphia, the pressure became overwhelming. She dropped out, moved to New York City, and began giving herself a self-directed dance education, taking up to four classes a day in widely different styles, including jazz, modern, tap, salsa, flamenco, belly-dancing, break-dancing, West African, pole dancing, and capoeira.

A year later, at age 20, Anne met a budding video producer, Jacob Krupnick, who was mesmerized by her hybrid dance style. He suggested that they collaborate on "something kind of gigantic."

When the DJ mash-up artist named Girl Talk released his newest album, titled *All Day*, Anne and Jacob realized they'd found their muse. Thus was born *Girl Walk // All Day*, an epic-length, 75-minute dance video scored to the entire Girl Talk album, broken into 12 individual videos, and made available for free online.

Now imagine you're someone like Anne Marsen. You don't have a college degree, and you want to audition for a new dance piece. What's the first thing you show people: your résumé or your incredible 75-minute dance video?

Which is more likely to make someone smile? Which will immediately communicate your style and experience as a dancer? And which will just be more fun?

The video, of course.

Highly effective self-directed learners don't just use the Internet to consume quality content; they also use it to share their passions, talents, thoughts, and projects.

Creating content carries three distinct advantages, no matter whether your content is a website, video, photo, blog, publicly viewable social media account, podcast, code, or application.

1. By creating something for an audience, you hold yourself to a higher standard. If Anne and Jacob were just making a dance video for themselves, would they have put in nearly as much effort? No way. We care more and try harder when we know something will be public.
2. When you create something for others, you effectively become a teacher, and teaching something prompts you to understand it more deeply.
3. Create enough content, and soon you'll have a digital paper trail: an online, googleable repository of real-world accomplishments and self-directed projects that people will find infinitely more interesting than an old-fashioned résumé.

Girl Walk // All Day succeeds because it makes people smile, but that's not the only metric for a successful online artifact. You can also make someone cry, help them think differently, or solve one of their problems. Sometimes the easiest way to start is to ask yourself, what content do I wish existed when I was trying to learn something online?

Future employers will google you; future romantic partners will google you; and your future kids might even google you, so start filling the Internet with your creations to leave a trail worth following.

LEARNING OFFLINE

12

Information
Versus
Knowledge

A common phrase I hear in alternative education circles today is, "You can learn *anything* online!"

Well, no. Now that we've discussed the wonderful and empowering features of the Internet, let's talk about its limitations.

Consider the story of Massive Online Open Courses (MOOCs). When MOOCs first appeared in 2006, critics heralded them as the end of traditional education. Harvard and MIT professors lecturing online for free? The doors to the Ivy League have been flung open! This will change everything!

But not much changed. In 2013, while thousands of people registered for individual MOOC courses, roughly 95% of them didn't complete the course, a dropout rate far worse than actual face-to-face courses. And needless to say, Harvard and MIT didn't go anywhere.

There are many reasons that people drop out of MOOCs, and the courses will certainly evolve, improve, and begin retaining more students. But the fact remains that most people don't want to listen to a college professor talk for hours on end, even from the comfort of their own rooms.

I believe the core reason that computers won't replace face-to-face instruction anytime soon is that there's a big difference between *information* and *knowledge*.

On the Internet you can access unlimited amounts of information: static data, text, videos, opinions, and analyses. Such information is important and useful to a point, but without context, it quickly becomes overwhelming. Anyone who has scrolled through 20+ pages of search results knows this feeling.

Knowledge, on the other hand, is when you connect the dots between different pieces of information, grasp the context, and see the big picture. Gaining knowledge feels like an "a-ha!" moment of clear understanding.

Here's the rub. While we can consume huge amounts of information by ourselves, we almost always need other, real-life human beings to help us connect the dots and build knowledge.

Not convinced? Try this: look for the answer to the question "What is love?" online.

Websites, videos, and MOOCs might be great places to start finding answers to this age-old question. But at some point, you'll need to get off the computer and throw yourself into a few actual relationships. Or talk to retired people about love and loss. Or take a camping trip with friends and get lost in conversation under the starry sky. To deepen your knowledge, you need interactions with real-life humans. Chat rooms do this poorly, videoconferencing does it better, but flesh-and-blood people are where the really deep learning happens.

What if you want to discuss the common themes of two lesser-known novels? Start with an online search, but then introduce yourself to bookstore owners. Go to a local book club, even if it's full of people 20 years your junior or senior. Drive across three states to join a gathering of fellow literary enthusiasts.

What if you want to figure out what makes one scientific study biased and another unbiased? Try finding an actual research scientist and inviting her out to tea. Track down the author of an article about confirmation bias. Do your own scientific study and watch yourself closely to see how enticing it is to skew the results.

If you're focusing entirely on computer skills like graphic design or programming, then yes, the Internet alone can take you very far. (YouTube tutorials are wonderful things.) But the best graphic designers and programmers still attend face-to-face conferences that provide the invaluable opportunities for deep connection that online forums cannot.

Real-life people communicate with body language. They understand subtle context. They build trust, assess character, and empathize: functions that computers cannot yet replicate with any success. That's why businesspeople still meet face-to-face to close big deals and the matching power of online dating sites is fundamentally limited. For the really important stuff, computers just don't beat face-to-face.

Humans still do much that computers cannot. Don't fall into the trap of thinking you can learn everything online.

13

Alone, Together

ALONE   ALONE-TOGETHER

Have you ever tried to write a novel? Yes? Then you know what soul-crushing despair looks like: you, sitting by yourself, in front of a blinking cursor.

Now imagine trying to write a novel as a teenager. Could you motivate yourself to finish an entire book at that age? To most, the prospect seems impossible.

But in 2009, as part of the first Unschool Adventures Writing Retreat, we brought 15 teenagers to a beach house in Oregon for a month and watched each of them write 50,000 words of original fiction.

We ran it again in Colorado with 20 teens. Then on Cape Cod with

25 teens. Every year, the teens—passionate but largely untrained amateurs—continued to write volumes.

What was the trick? Did we intensively coach the teens or closely monitor their daily word counts? Did we outlaw non-writing-related socializing, make them go to bed early to ensure sufficient rest, require attendance at all workshops and group activities, or use some more complex trick to motivate them to work toward their challenging goals?

We did none of these things.

The secret to the success of the Writing Retreat, I believe, was that we created a place for our writers to work alone, together.

Here's a little slice of life at the Writing Retreat. Imagine waking up in a bunk bed to the smell of toasting bagels, stumbling into a common area, and seeing four people typing dutifully on their laptops. What seems like the logical thing to do? Start writing.

But let's say you don't. Instead, you to opt to take a walk on the beach. Passing by the local coffee shop on the way back, you run into two more fellow students, each writing. What seems like the logical thing to do? Write.

Or maybe you don't. Instead, you return to the house, where you find a "power hour" underway, a fun challenge to see who can write the most words in an hour. Or a writing workshop about plot lines. Or a casual conversation about character development. What do you do next? Well, you probably start writing.

At the Writing Retreat, no matter where you go, some form of writing is happening. People are working on their individual books, but they're doing it together. In this kind of culture, writing is simply what you do. It's as natural as breathing.

Then, suddenly, it's the end of the month, and you've written 50,000 words, but with far less pain and suffering than if you'd attempted it on your own.

Self-directed learners often find themselves facing solitary challenges, simply because they're not doing the same thing as everyone else. Then they give themselves a hard time for not feeling motivated.

But self-directed learning isn't about doing everything by yourself. Putting yourself in the right atmosphere, with people who share your interests, and with the right amount of structure, can make all the difference.

When the challenge of individual work feels overwhelming, join a community of people facing the same challenge.

Humans are pack creatures. If you put us in solitary confinement we go insane. This is generally true even for introverted people; only on the far edge of the bell curve do you find people who crave absolute solitude for weeks or months on end (and these people tend to be really odd, and it's often hard to tell if the oddness is cause or effect).

However . . . being surrounded by a bunch of people that is constantly interrupting you makes it hard to focus. And so civic design has evolved the library, the coffee shop, and the co-working space: Places where you can be alone yet also surrounded by people.

The secret is to surround yourself with people who don't have the same agenda as you. Then you won't often be interrupted by things that break your focus: The staff might occasionally ask to refill your coffee, and you'll get interrupted if the building catches fire, but otherwise you can work on your own thing.

—Michael F. Booth commenting on a *Hacker News* post

Nerd Clans

When I was a freshman at the University of California at Berkeley, I lived in a 125-person cooperative house called Casa Zimbabwe. Unlike in traditional college dorms, the members of Casa Zimbabwe did everything themselves—cooking, cleaning, and managing—in exchange for a lower rent and a more lively atmosphere.

I started my co-op career as an assistant cook, stir-frying foot-high piles of veggies and tofu in massive steel containers. Then I became a head cook, planning dinners to satisfy omnivores, vegetarians, and vegans alike. As my skills and passion for cooking grew, I soon became part of the Casa Zimbabwe food mafia: an informal group of fellow cooks and epicures who challenged each other to create better and fancier dinners.

At the end of every semester, Casa Zimbabwe held a food party called Special Dinner. Unfortunately, the event had long been a sterile affair catered by an overpriced Italian food company. The food mafia and I decided to transform Special Dinner into something worthy of its name.

We began by replacing the caterers with our own in-house cooks. Then we held a half-dozen menu brainstorming meetings that resulted in dishes like Goat Cheese and Leek Galette, Roasted Rib Steak with Chanterelles, and Meyer Lemon Sorbet with Fresh Berries. We convinced the house social managers to redecorate the dining area in the theme of an enchanted forest, complete with freshly trimmed tree foliage gathered from landscaping sites and violin performances by local buskers. We promoted the event passionately at house meetings in order to draw everyone, including the most studious and antisocial house members, to the event.

The result of our efforts: a seven-course, 27-dish, four-hour-long revel in which our house community feasted, partied, and bonded like never before.

The next semester, inspired by the success of the Special Dinner, the food mafia and I helped reinvent another stale house party, the Dessert Party, rechristening it as a "Bacchanalia." That evening we presented the house with large platters of finger foods and bowls of melted chocolate, and we gave everyone just one rule: you're not allowed to feed yourself. Unsurprisingly, we all ended up covered in chocolate.

When I finished my time at Berkeley, I felt ready to leave academia, but I was incredibly sad to leave my cherished college nerd clan.

A nerd cares so much about his quirky interests, projects, or hobbies, that he has no time to play popularity games. Nerds bond quickly with other nerds because they choose to focus on building stuff, learning stuff, and otherwise "nerding out" rather than clawing up a social hierarchy.

In high school, being a nerd was a liability. Caring too much about something was the fast track to social exclusion. But in Casa Zimbabwe (and U.C. Berkeley in general), caring deeply was the fast track to making close friends.

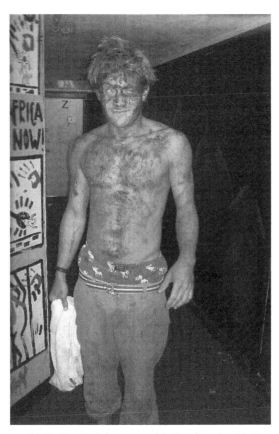

Blake in Casa Zimbabwe, covered in chocolate, circa 2002

As a self-directed learner who cared passionately about many things, living in Casa Zimbabwe helped me realize that there was only one way for me to build a social life: by embracing my nerd-hood and actively seeking other nerds. By maintaining that attitude, I found and joined many nerd clans that I'm still part of today: the international traveler clan, the summer camp clan, and the alternative educator clan.

To find your nerd clans, seek out people who are excited to do the kind of work that makes most others cringe (in my case: cook for groups of 90, travel the world with only a small backpack, or live outside working with kids all summer). Start by looking for preexisting self-selected communities like workplaces, colleges, online groups, and hobbyist groups.

If those don't exist, then just focus on finding one or two people who share your passion. Propose a shared project (like co-creating a big meal), challenge each other to go farther than you would have on your own, and then revel in the bliss of nerd-hood.

To build a social life as a self-directed learner, seek out pockets of fellow enthusiasts with infectious self-motivation.

Being a nerd, which is to say going too far and caring too much about a subject, is the best way to make friends I know. For me, the spark that turns an acquaintance into a friend has usually been kindled by some shared enthusism like detective novels or Ulysses S. Grant.

—Sarah Vowell, *The Partly Cloudy Patriot*

META-LEARNING

15

Learning How to Learn

I once led a six-week leadership retreat for five self-directed learners ages 18–21. I rented them an apartment in the bustling town of Ashland, Oregon, helped them devise a clear set of learning goals for the retreat, and mentored them toward completing those goals using the approaches described in this book.

One student wanted to learn about biology and Kendo; another wanted to improve her photography and web design skills. So I sent them away to interview biologists, martial arts instructors, photographers, and designers. My students boldly introduced themselves to complete strangers, pushed themselves to learn both online and offline, and then blogged about their successes and failures, over and over again.

Those were just the weekdays. On the weekends, I sent the students out on wild adventures to build their self-directed resolve in some rather unusual ways.

For "hobo weekend," they hiked on train tracks (on which trains weren't actually running) to the local reservoir and camped out under tarps and thin blankets, a lesson in the importance of maintaining one's attitude in a difficult situation: like not having a home to return to at night.

For "travel weekend," I challenged teams of students to get as far away from our home base as possible, and back, in 48 hours with only $50. I showed them how to use the websites Craigslist (to find cheap rideshares) and Couchsurfing (to find free housing), gave them some safety protocols, and then sent them on their way. One team made it as far as San Francisco, a 700-mile round-trip.

For "entrepreneur weekend," the students attempted to earn as much money as possible using only $5 seed capital. For "paperclip weekend," they traded up a worthless starting object (a paperclip) into a more valuable one (a set of golf clubs) using only their wits.

For the final weekend, I gave them surprise one-way tickets on a Portland-bound Amtrak train, a to-do list with tasks drawn from previous retreat activities, and the challenge to eat, sleep, and get themselves back four days later, with a budget of only $80 each. (My program co-leader, Cameron, also boarded the train, trailing the group undetected with a fake moustache, as an extra safety measure.) Spoiler alert: they made it.

Walking the mean streets of Portland, Oregon. (Photo: Trevor Parker)

When the program ended, everyone went home happy—and I spent a long time asking myself why I ran it.

My leadership retreat combined some of the most fun and interesting activities I'd picked up over my years of hanging around innovative summer camps, Silicon Valley entrepreneurs, world travelers, and outdoor educators. I hadn't thought about how they fit together before I ran the program, but there had to be a common thread. What was it?

An excerpt from a blog post by the author Seth Godin finally nailed the answer for me:

> *An organization filled with honest, motivated, connected, eager, learning, experimenting, ethical and driven people will always defeat the one that merely has talent. Every time.*

The world is full of places that try to teach "talent," school and college being the preeminent two. But the world has far fewer places that attempt to teach honesty, motivation, ethics, and the other traits Godin described.

Yet for many businesses and other enterprises, these traits ultimately matter more than talent. People get hired for professional skills and fired for personal skills.

That's when I realized that what I was teaching at the leadership retreat was what educators call *meta-learning*: the personal skills that help you learn effectively in complex and unpredictable environments.

The leadership retreat wasn't really about sleeping under a tarp or finding rideshares or learning biology or Kendo: it was about building resourcefulness, creativity, self-regulation, self-motivation, conscientiousness, and focus. It was about greeting a stranger, learning from a defeat, arguing one's case, and telling a good story. Meta-learning was the thread that connected all of my own formative educational experiences, and I was trying to pass that thread along.

The best teachers, mentors, and organizations don't just pour information into your head; they teach the meta-learning skills that help you learn how to learn. To find them, look for anyone who will teach you how to:

- give and take feedback
- speak in front of people
- tell a powerful story
- write something that people actually want to read
- lead a group
- follow in a group
- make a decent movie, website, or photograph
- live on a budget
- spot logical fallacies in an argument
- meet and converse with anyone
- set a goal and follow through on it

Seek out the teachers, coaches, and mentors in life who prefer to teach you how to fish instead of simply giving you a fish.

16

The Dance Lesson

Blake, touch my chest!"

The 50-year-old Argentine woman spoke with authority, so I did as she commanded.

I placed my palms on her clavicles. As she walked forward, I held the tension in my arms and walked backwards, matching my steps to hers.

When she paused, I paused. When she twisted her torso or shifted weight in her feet, I followed.

The year was 2008, I was 26, and I was leading my first Unschool Adventures trip to Argentina. Ostensibly, Alicia Pons was teaching my group of teens how to dance tango, using me, for a moment, to demonstrate the art of following. (Argentine tango is composed of leader and follower pairs.) But clearly, something more than tango was happening here.

"As a leader, you need to send clear signals," Alicia instructed us. "You must know what you want and move decisively. Otherwise, your partner won't know how to respond."

For a moment, I felt like I was in a relationship therapy session.

"If you don't know what you want, then stop moving. Just shift the weight in your feet for a few moments. That's okay." Alicia rocked back and forth almost imperceptibly; I felt the motions in her chest and moved my body to match.

Now it was a life coaching session.

"In the early days of Argentine tango," she continued, "every man had to learn how to follow—to listen very carefully—before he could become a leader, before he could take that responsibility. Today, we have many bad leaders because they've never followed before."

Now: a communication class (and political theory, too).

She released me and entered the middle of the tiny dance studio. "No matter whether you're leading or following, you must walk confidently. Raise your arms high above your head and take a deep breath. Then keep your chest in that position as you release your arms. Feel your spine lengthen. Feel your new height. This is how you will connect with your partner in tango. Practice walking like this everywhere you go."

The basics of body language? Alicia just summarized them.

"At a *milonga* (a social tango dance), it's common to dance four songs together. If you begin dancing with a partner, you are committing to all four songs. It's rude to leave early, but you always have the power to say no. If your partner is being disrespectful, walk away immediately."

Finally, a lesson about consent.

For two weeks in Buenos Aires, Alicia taught my group more than just tango—she taught us how to move with confidence, power, and grace while remaining humble, perceptive, and open to feedback. Having danced, competed, and taught across the world, Alicia had an incredible repertoire of moves to show us, but she focused entirely on one lesson: communication.

• • •

Self-directed learners need to confidently and clearly communicate with other real-life human beings, not just computer screens. We need to advocate for our nontraditional paths to parents, employers, or college admissions officers. We need to work successfully with teammates and coworkers. We need to ask smart questions, ask for help, and stand up for ourselves.

But none of these communication tasks is easy or automatic, and some are downright terrifying.

What I discovered in Buenos Aires was that partner dancing is just one big communication lesson that teaches a set of interpersonal skills that you could never get from a book, classroom, or website.

I learned my lesson via Argentine tango, but I have friends who gained just as much insight from swing dancing and blues dancing.

Do yourself a favor and google partner dancing classes in your area, right now. Tango, swing, blues, ballroom—the specific form doesn't matter as long as it involves improvisation, not just choreographed steps. Go alone or with a friend, whatever makes you more comfortable. Take a few classes and try different teachers. When you find the right one, you'll know, because all of a sudden you won't just be learning dance anymore. You'll be learning to kick more butt at life itself.

Learn to dance, and dance to learn. It's all about communication.

17

Indescribable Sexiness

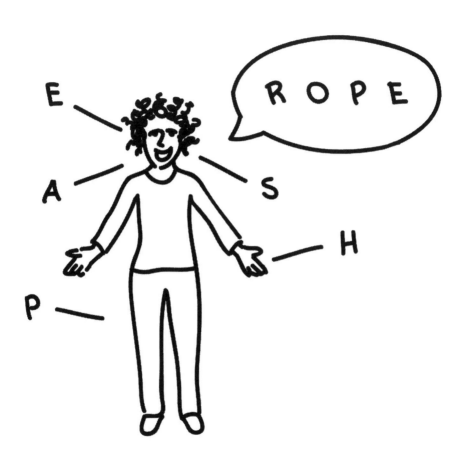

When I present at homeschooling conferences, my most popular teen workshop is called *Indescribable Sexiness*, a crash course in meeting and conversing with strangers.

Go ahead, I know what you're thinking. "Oh, those poor unsocialized homeschoolers."

But I don't lead this workshop because homeschoolers are too awkward to talk to each other. (They're no more awkward than other teens.) I do it because it's the advice I wish somebody had given me when I was their age.

Here's the workshop in a nutshell.

Did you know that there are two types of sexiness? The first kind is the skin-deep attractiveness of movie stars and models, and you're pretty much born with it or not. The second is a set a body language and conversation tools that anyone can pick up and practice: tools that give you a hard-to-define, *indescribable* sexiness.

The first acronym for indescribable sexiness is PASHE, which describes five things to do in order to make a good first impression. Why do first impressions matter? Because people judge books by their covers. That's not to say that people are shallow—they're just practical. Have you ever been to a bookstore? Of course you judge books by their covers. The same goes for meeting people.

P is for posture. Stand up tall, leaving your arms hanging at your sides. Breathe deeply.

A is for amplify. Have you ever noticed how far your ear is from your mouth, and then how far everyone else's ears are from your mouth? We need to talk a little louder than we typically assume in order to be heard. Very quiet speech is a-w-k-w-a-r-d.

S is for smile. Try this: completely relax your facial muscles, then look in the mirror. Most of us see a frown, or at least something not very inviting. Our faces don't smile naturally. When you meet someone, remember to smile with both your eyes (creating "crow's feet") and your teeth.

H is for hands. When people are nervous, their hands show it by fidgeting with their clothing, resting against a nearby object, or hiding in their pockets or armpits. Take your hands out and simply leave them by your sides. If you shake someone's hand, use simple, firm pressure, avoiding both the "limp fish" and "bodybuilder" extremes.

E is for eye contact. Eye contact is important, but too much or too little is a problem. If you only hold eye contact for a fraction of a second, you seem nervous. But if you hold eye contact for too long—especially with someone you just met—you send an equally undesirable message. Give someone three to five seconds of eye contact at a time, and if you're talking to a group, spread your gaze around evenly instead of just focusing on one person.

After introducing my workshop attendees to PASHE, I have the teens form a long line and practice meeting each other using PASHE. Then I have them turn all the letters off, to feel the clear sensation of awkwardness. Finally I have them turn on all the letters except one, meet each other, and try to guess which letter their partners had turned off. (Most of us have one or two letters that we need to improve upon.)

The second tool for indescribable sexiness is ROPE: four tools for creating conversation. This is how you take an interaction beyond first impressions.

R is for reflective listening. A technique commonly employed by therapists, this is how you show somebody that you're *really* listening to them instead of just *acting like* you're listening. The exercise begins with teens speaking short sentences and repeating them back to each other verbatim. Then they do it again, changing only one or two key words. The new words must mean the same thing. For example, if someone tells you, "I had a bad day," you can repeat back to them, "You had a terrible day," but not,

"You had a bad week." Finally, the teens string together multiple sentences of reflective listening to create a mini-conversation that proves they're actually listening.

O is for open-ended questions. Reflective listening can't take you very far in a conversation. To keep people talking (or take a conversation in a new direction), ask an open-ended question, one that has multiple possible answers. For example, some open-ended questions you might ask me would be, "What makes you want to continue working with homeschoolers?" or "Why do you love online cat videos so much?"

P is for personal statements. So far, our conversation tactics have been entirely about the other person. But injecting your own thoughts and opinions is important. Continuing our previous conversation, perhaps you would add, "I think cat videos are pretty stupid and a waste of space on the Internet." And then I would say, "I humbly disagree," and then go back to open-ended questions, asking you, "What kind of stupid animal videos do you prefer?"

E is for experiences: a reminder that the best conversations end with concrete experiences—i.e., *doing stuff*—instead of just talking. "Hey, let's go see a movie!" or "Hey, let's go make our own cat video!" If you like the person you're talking to, don't be afraid to actually go and do something with her instead of just talking forever.

To have a great conversation with anyone in the world, all you have to do is PASHE 'em and ROPE 'em.

18

Deliberate Practice

Armed with a high-speed Internet connection, a self-directed learner can introduce herself to virtually any subject on earth. She can learn a little about a lot of different things. But what happens when she wants to obtain mastery? Can she accomplish this on her own, or does she need something more?

A fascinating 1991 experiment by Dr. K. Anders Ericsson, a psychologist who studies the acquisition of expert skills, sheds light on the answer.

In the experiment, Ericsson took his research team to the Music Academy of West Berlin, which was famous for producing world-class violinists, and asked the Academy's professors to separate their students into three categories:

1. top violinists (those who might become international soloists)
2. good violinists (those who might join the top symphony orchestras)
3. okay violinists (those who might become music teachers)

Ericsson's team then interviewed the students about their musical careers, asking them when they started playing, how many hours a week they practiced, and how they specifically went about their practice.

At first, the data revealed surprising similarities. Students from all three groups had been studying violin for at least a decade, and each spent roughly 51 hours in combined weekly lessons, solo practice, and classes at the Music Academy. From these numbers alone, it was impossible to predict who would become a top violinist.

But as the researchers dug deeper into the students' interviews, something interesting surfaced. It turned out that the Academy's top violinists were doing a totally different type of practice from everyone else, a type of practice that wasn't fun or lighthearted, but hard, challenging, and unpleasant. Ericsson began calling this specific type of work *deliberate practice*.

Ericsson's team also discovered that, while all the violinists did a similar amount of practice at the academy, the more talented ones had accumulated significantly more deliberate practice earlier in their lives. By age 18, the top violinists had spent an average of 7,410 total lifetime hours doing deliberate practice; the second group, 5,301 hours; the third group, 3,420.

Apparently doing deliberate practice, and doing a lot of it, was the road to mastery.

As other researchers began studying deliberate practice, they discovered that it didn't just apply to music but also to chess, sports, science, business, and pretty much any other tangible, measurable skill.

Here's how deliberate practice (DP) differs from regular practice:

- DP requires that you know exactly what you want to achieve. For example: "I want to play this specific riff from my favorite song," not, "I want to get better at the guitar."
- DP is designed to nudge you just past your current level of performance. The practice can be divided into bite-sized chunks—not too hard, not too easy—that meet your exact challenge level.
- DP is repeatable. You can work on each chunk over and over again until you've got it down cold.
- During DP, performance feedback is constantly available. Someone knowledgeable is monitoring your progress and can tell you how you're doing.
- DP is mentally demanding. No one can do it for more than four or five hours a day.
- When you're doing DP, it's not much fun. It's strenuous and painful.

Self-directed learning typically begins with a lot of exploratory solo learning: reading books, working on computers, or quietly contemplating, for example. These approaches work well for building surface-level skills. But when she is ready to go beyond the surface and start developing mastery in a subject, a self-directed learner must find an experienced and dedicated human helper to create an environment of deliberate practice.

Deliberate practice is the heart of what the best schools, colleges, coaches, training programs, and camps provide. For example, why is Oxford University's tutorial system, in which students meet with professors directly in groups of only two or three, held in such high regard? Because its intimacy and direct feedback sets the stage for deliberate practice.

Why, in the digital age, does virtually everyone acknowledge the value of an old-school carpentry apprenticeship? Because we understand that repetitive, hands-on practice under the guidance of a master is a timeless method for developing expertise.

Why, as a young camper at Deer Crossing Camp, did I voluntarily don a wetsuit and jump into a freezing-cold mountain lake in order to take windsurfing classes? Because I relished the rapid learning that resulted from the camp's deliberate practice-style teaching techniques. (And that's why I went back to become a windsurfing instructor, too.)

Self-directed learners (like everyone else) tend to avoid deliberate practice at first, because it's hard, scary, and time-consuming. But once you've tasted the fruit of its process—true mastery—then you know its value. Any self-directed learner who embraces and purposefully seeks out deliberate practice becomes a learning powerhouse.

When looking for deliberate practice experience, don't be afraid to start with the most traditional and structured places of learning. More often than not, when a martial arts dojo, dance studio, or graduate school has a good reputation, it's because they do a good job with deliberate practice.

For those without the time, money, or inclination to join a

formal organization, another way to do deliberate practice is by directly recruiting a freelance teacher, tutor, mentor, or coach to provide the experience. Find this person online, through a local organization, or through a friend's referral.

No matter where you look for a deliberate practice coach, heed the excellent advice of researcher and author Daniel Coyle:

Avoid someone who reminds you of a courteous waiter. People who want to keep you forever comfortable, happy, and unburdened make great restaurant waiters, but terrible coaches for deliberate practice.

Seek someone who scares you a little, someone who watches you closely, prefers jumping into activities over extensive talking, and gives unnervingly honest feedback.

Seek someone who gives short, clear directions. No sermons, no lectures—just short, unmistakably clear directions that guide you to a target.

Seek someone who loves teaching fundamentals. They may spend an entire session focusing on one small detail.

Other things being equal, pick the older person. Teaching is like any other talent: It takes time to grow.

To go from surface-level skills to deep mastery, find the people and places that can push you farther than you could ever push yourself.

SELF-DIRECTED EARNING

19

Pumping Poop for the Win

One of my longest-held goals is to start my own camp, alternative school, or other big, long-term, life-changing program for young adults.

It's an intimidating dream, because it will require a huge amount of dedication, commitment, money, and—of course—self-directed learning on my part.

Luckily, I have two excellent role models who each started their own summer camp: Grace Llewellyn, the founder of Not Back to School Camp, and Jim Wiltens, the founder of Deer Crossing Camp.

Throughout my twenties, as I worked at both of their camps,

I picked Grace's and Jim's brains about how they turned their camp dreams into realities. I loved both of their stories, but only Grace's had been documented at that time (in the beginning of her wonderful and timeless book, *The Teenage Liberation Handbook*).

Jim's story proved more elusive to piece together, and I made it my mission to unearth it, interviewing him as we led teen backpacking trips in the California High Sierra, at his home in Silicon Valley, and as we rode mules together through the Guatemalan jungle (with howler monkeys swinging overhead) on a tree-climbing and ruins expedition.

What I discovered wasn't just relevant to camp enthusiasts like myself, but an inspiring tale for any self-directed learner with a big dream that will require some challenging, frustrating, and sometimes dirty work to realize.

• • •

When Jim Wiltens was 14, his mother told him that if he wanted to go to college, he would have to work to contribute to his own college fund. An avid swimmer and water polo player, Jim decided to start a swim school in his backyard pool, giving away free lessons to neighborhood kids until he became popular enough to charge for his time. It turned out he didn't need the money, however, because a water polo scholarship funded his college degrees in biology and botany.

By the end of graduate school, Jim realized that he loved working for himself, coaching sports, and being in the outdoors so much that, when his mother proposed the idea of starting a family-owned children's summer camp, he said yes.

The family made their first attempt in Hawaii, where they found a former banana plantation that looked like a beautiful site for a camp, but after a year of red tape and island politics, they abandoned the possibility. They moved back to California, Jim moved into a tent in his parents' backyard to save money, and the search continued.

Luck struck again with the discovery of a 40-acre ranch in the far northern part of California that looked like a serious possibility. To live closer to the property, Jim used his untouched college fund to buy a small house in the nearby city of Redding, and he took a job at a lakefront resort to continue saving money.

His first job at the resort? Pumping poop from houseboats.

Most people with two college degrees would have felt that such a job was beneath them. But Jim didn't, because his parents raised him to think of every job as an opportunity to develop his perseverance, work ethic, and focus. He learned to always work for himself—even when employed, and even when the work was unpleasant. "When I pump poop," Jim told himself, "I want to be the best poop pumper in the world."

But even well-intentioned poop pumpers don't get breaks sometimes.

The Wiltens family was close to securing the business permits they needed when they discovered that certain local "horticultural interests" (i.e., marijuana farmers) didn't like the idea of local health department officials entering their area. False rumors began spreading that the new camp would be for juvenile delinquents. At the planning commission meeting, hundreds of audience members yelled at Jim and his family, "Flatlanders go home!" Needless to say, they didn't receive the permits.

Disappointed by this setback, Jim sold his house in Redding, moved back to the San Francisco Bay Area, and put his science background to use as a water purification chemist. The family felt close to giving up the summer camp dream, but Jim kept saving money for the possibility.

A realtor familiar with the family's search kept calling Jim's mother, telling her about a former Boy Scout camp near Lake Tahoe. Highly skeptical but curious, the family decided to drive up to see the camp.

What they discovered was an old lakefront lodge, with broken windows, that had been abandoned by the Boy Scouts due to extreme difficulty of operation. In flickering lantern light, Jim found a hundred old camp mattresses that an army of rats had claimed to build floor-to-ceiling nests. Dark things scurried back and forth between the piles. As Jim plunged a shovel into the first pile, a startled rat scrambled up the handle and leaped on Jim's back. Like a mini rodeo star, the rat held tight as Jim bucked and swirled around the room.

While the scout camp was a total wreck, the nearest neighbors (and thus any possible "horticultural" or other interests) were 17 miles away. The water pumping and purification system froze each winter, but Jim's background in underwater construction (another job he held at the poop-pumping resort) and water treatment could solve that. The Forest Service was open to another children's camp making use of the site—nobody had been bold (or stupid) enough to try.

The Wiltenses bought the property.

Thus began the Wiltens family weekend ritual in which the entire family (dogs included) piled into a station wagon, drove four hours, and hiked into the camp at night. Teaching themselves plumbing and carpentry, the family gutted and rebuilt the lodge by lantern light. During a freak storm, they climbed 20-foot ladders to install giant window panes before the lodge filled with snow. Every Monday they returned to their jobs in the San Francisco Bay Area, exhausted but happy.

Two years later, the climactic moment arrived. The family huddled together and, with one finger, Jim depressed a toilet handle. It flushed. This meant all the systems were finally working together: electricity, water pumps, and plumbing. They did a victory dance in the bathroom. The next summer, Deer Crossing Camp was born.

• • •

What I learned from Jim Wiltens was, if you have a big dream for which there is no clear blueprint, you will need self-directed learning.

You will suffer setbacks in the pursuit of your dream. You'll meet dead ends. And sometimes, you'll need to pump poop (hopefully metaphorical) to make it happen.

But as long as you're working for yourself, using every opportunity as a way to advance your dream, the setbacks and dead ends will be manageable.

To make your biggest dreams happen: embrace setbacks, take the dirty jobs when you must, and always work for yourself.

20

Passion, Skill, Market

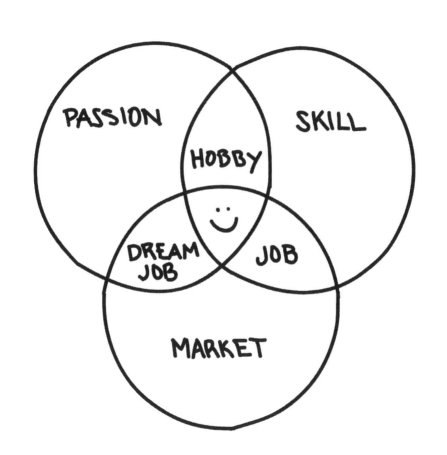

Carsie Blanton grew up in rural Virginia where she played on the rolling grassy hills, hunted salamanders, read books, and fiddled around with musical instruments. Seeing a happy and engaged child, Carsie's parents decided to simply never send her to school. They supported Carsie's interests, made her part of adult discussions at the house, and gave her large blocks of undisturbed personal time.

At 13, Carsie discovered a deep love for guitar and songwriting. At 16, she moved to Oregon to join a group house with other artists, where she met a funk band who invited her to sing backup and tour the United States. As she traveled, she began building her own body of musical work.

In her twenties, Carsie independently recorded and released a few albums, leading to new gigs and a few big breaks (like opening for Paul Simon). She worked in coffee shops to pay the bills before her shows and CD sales became profitable.

Instead of going to college, she trained with top musicians, struck up friendships with interesting people she met on the road, and continued her lifelong habit of reading lots of hard books. She fell in love with swing dancing, started taking swing classes whenever possible, and eventually began teaching her own classes.

Then, at age 28, Carsie mobilized her fans on Kickstarter with the goal of raising $29,000 to produce a new jazz album, offering preorders of the album, personalized songwriting, and other interesting rewards in exchange for donations.

She hit her target and then kept going, all the way to $60,000, enough to produce her album, pay a few big-name jazz musicians to contribute, hire a publicity team, *and* take her entire band on tour across the United States.

• • •

Running a Kickstarter campaign is essentially like starting a business in an incredibly short time span: you've got to develop a product, create a compelling story, attract an audience, and then deliver. Like most business startups, most online fundraising campaigns fail. But Carsie, an unschooled young woman with no formal training, nailed it on the first try. How?

Having traveled, performed, and danced all across the United States, Carsie had built one heck of a social network, an important element for fundraising success. But I don't think that was the main thing.

Carsie carefully planned her fundraising campaign, studied other musicians' campaigns, and asked for lots of feedback before going live. Those actions certainly helped, but I still don't think they explain everything.

Instead, I believe that Carsie received an early and powerful education in applying her self-directed learning to the needs of others.

With all of our talk about *self*-directed learning, it's easy to assume that our educations should focus only on ourselves. But people who, like Carsie, want their hobbies to fund their lives know that focusing only on yourself is the fast path to going broke. Instead, we must take what we love and figure out how to use it to inform, entertain, educate, or help other people.

Tina Seelig of the Stanford Design School masterfully explains the idea with the threefold concept of passion, skill, and market.

- If you're passionate about something, but you're not skilled in it, then you're a fan. (Think, for example, of a beginning guitar enthusiast.)
- If you're passionate about something *and* skilled in it, then you've got a hobby. (Think of a guitarist with some training and experience.)
- If you're skilled in something, there's a market for it, but you don't have any passion for it, then you have a job. (Think of a guitarist who is good enough to play gigs, but he lost his love for guitar long ago.)

Combine all three elements—passion, skills, and a market—and you arrive at Mecca: meaningful work that also pays the bills. (Think of a musician, like Carsie, who loves playing gigs and can make a living doing it.)

Self-directed learners are typically very good at identifying their passions. They build skills when necessary. But finding (or creating) a market? That's the hard part, because it means they must stop thinking only about themselves and start trying to understand other people.

Understanding the needs of other people, I propose, is exactly what Carsie was doing in her adventure-filled youth.

Playing music shows? An exercise in discovering other people's tastes.

Working in coffee shops? An exercise in providing value to an employer.

Teaching swing dance lessons? An exercise in helping people learn something complex.

By paying close attention to the needs of others while also building her skills and deepening her passions, Carsie created a self-directed education that wasn't just about herself. So when it came time to launch her Kickstarter campaign, she didn't make the rookie mistake of focusing on me, me, me. Instead, she created something that other people actually wanted.

Do what you love, but also keep an eye on the needs of others—that's how self-directed learning can turn into self-directed earning.

Living life without school is not the easy way out. It's a lot like self-employment. It's a great way to live, but it's not for everyone. When self-directed learning gets hard, some teens feel like adults who say, "Can I just have my 40-hour per week job back?"

—Ken Danford, co-founder of
North Star: Self-Directed Learning for Teens

21

Time
Wealth

INCOME − EXPENSES

= TIME

My friend Dev Carey, age 50, lives on the Western Slope of Colorado, just outside the tiny town of Paonia. Surrounded by sage, juniper, and a sweeping view of the valley below, he lives in a 2-bedroom, naturally built straw-bale home that he and friends constructed for under $30,000.

With rainwater cisterns, solar panels, and a composting toilet, Dev lives almost entirely off the grid. He pays no utilities, no mortgage, and minimal property tax. He cooks his own food, lends a hand to neighboring farmers in exchange for portions of their crops, and unschools his 11-year-old daughter, Seraya. As a lifelong educator, Dev, who has a PhD in ecology, frequently hosts former students who are passing through the area.

How much money does Dev need to support this lifestyle? Approximately $15,000 per year (including health insurance and savings): a sum that he easily cobbles together with a few short-term jobs like adventure-trip-leading, counseling, teaching private high school classes, or working for a conservation district.

Dev's life isn't wealthy in the conventional sense, but it's incredibly wealthy in terms of *time*.

If the weather forecast shows a beautiful week ahead, Dev can take the time to climb a nearby mountain, hike the Grand Canyon, or explore the Canyonlands of Utah. If he's craving some Spanish practice, he can pop into Northern Mexico and visit the small house on an onion field that he purchased for $800. If he wants to organize a kid's camp or invite some former students on a hitchhiking adventure, he can do it. When a friend calls seeking life advice, Dev stays on the phone for two hours. And when a neighbor needs help with a big harvest, he's the first to volunteer.

Dev enjoys a level of freedom that many people earning more can only dream about. Why? Because he keeps his expenses low, works intensively in short bursts to pay his bills, and then stops working (for money, at least) as soon as the bills are paid.

Most importantly, Dev has carefully considered what's important and what's not in his life. He knows that the time he spends helping his neighbors, adventuring with friends, mentoring former students, and learning with his daughter are what really matter. More paid work wouldn't buy him more of these experiences.

You probably don't want to live off the grid in Western Colorado like Dev—that's reasonable. But you could undoubtedly follow his lead by thinking hard about what's most important in your life, figuring out exactly how much that costs, and then reducing the amount of time you work, ultimately creating more time for friends, family, travel, adventure, and self-directed learning.

Time is money, but that doesn't mean you need to make more money to have more free time.

22

Career Advice from a Robot Dinosaur

Have you ever met a fake giant robot dinosaur?

Neither had I, until I met Fake Grimlock.

Fake Grimlock is a Twitter personality (@FAKEGRIMLOCK) who dispenses wisdom in 140-character bursts—always with ALL-CAPS and poor grammar—for tech entrepreneurs and anyone else who is building something from scratch.

A few example tweets include:

> STARTUPS BUILD TOMORROW FROM ASHES OF TODAY.
> THAT GREAT FOR EVERYONE BUT THE ASHES.

EVERYONE WISH THERE A MAGIC PILL FOR BE AWESOME.
THERE IS. IT CALLED "HARD WORK."

Grimlock also illustrates:

Courtesy @FAKEGRIMLOCK via Creative Commons

The most interesting part about @FAKEGRIMLOCK is that the account is anonymous. Virtually no one knows who writes the tweets, yet it has more than 10,000 followers.

How did this happen? As the author of the account revealed in a rare out-of-persona interview:

> *Nobody knew who I was. I used none of my connections. I didn't leverage my friends. Absolutely started from scratch, just randomly on Twitter. [I] followed a few people, and a few people followed me. . . . I realized there is an audience in the tech world that I can reach. . . . That I can come from nowhere, hack the social channel, and become an authority in tech, with nothing. Purely just because what I say is true.*

Grimlock's story illustrates the idea that in order to carve your own career path in the world, you need to:

1. find a group of people in the world who you understand
2. create something that they find useful, inspiring, or entertaining

Do these two things, and people will gladly give you their money or attention. That's the basic promise of entrepreneurship.

But the story of our robot dinosaur friend also illustrates a more valuable lesson, that creating a useful product—whether it's an article, video, sandwich, computer game, designer baby clothes, tech widget, or whatever else—may not be sufficient for success.

To really kick butt in this world, your product needs to have a personality behind it.

Here's how Fake Grimlock—a living example of this concept in action—explains it:

WHEN CHOOSE PRODUCT, HUMANS ONLY CARE ABOUT DOES WORK, AND IS INTERESTING.

WORLD ALREADY FULL OF THINGS DO WORK. MOST BORING.

PERSONALITY = INTERESTING. INTERESTING = CARE.
CARE = TALK.

EVERYONE CARE AND TALK ABOUT PRODUCT? YOU WIN.

Grimlock emphasizes that whatever you build needs to be quality. "Does it work?" is an important question. But in a world with many different quality products to choose from, the next question becomes, "Why should anyone care about this?" That's where personality steps in.

In a bacon sandwich, for example, both the bread and bacon are important for the sandwich to work, but the bacon is the personality.

To have a personality, Grimlock argues, you must answer three questions:

1. How you change customer's life?
2. What you stand for?

3. Who or what you hate?

If you can answer these questions—and convey the answers in the product you create—then people will want to buy what you're selling.

Grimlock's advice makes me think of my time in college around age 20. If someone had asked me at that moment why I was studying astrophysics, I would have told them that stars are interesting, and that's pretty much it.

The more complete truth was that I got good grades in my math and science classes in high school; *astrophysicist* was an ego-stroking title, and astrophysics just seemed more interesting than anything else I might be doing at the time.

The "product" I was creating at that time—expertise in math and science—didn't have much of a personality behind it. If I had continued that path, I don't think I would have ended up a very successful research scientist.

Luckily, in the middle of earning my college degree, I discovered alternative education, and all of a sudden, I had found my personality.

> *How did I intend to change people's lives?* By showing them new and exciting educational paths outside of the traditional route.

> *What did I stand for?* Taking full responsibility for one's education and life.

> *Who or what did I hate?* The wasting of young people's time in compulsory schooling when there were so many other engaging, productive, and enjoyable things they could be doing.

My newfound personality made my next choices clear: quit astrophysics, design my own major, and get involved in as many alternative and experiential education programs as possible. It also got people interested in me, asking why I abandoned a seemingly fruitful track through university to join a tie-dyed clan of unschoolers, or why I supported the legal right to homeschool when I didn't share the religious beliefs that motivated many homeschoolers.

Having a personality behind my product, I believe, was the true key to my modest self-directed career successes as a young adult: getting my first book published, getting paid to speak at education conferences, and starting Unschool Adventures.

Today, I still need to make things that people actually want. Having a personality doesn't make up for bad products. I've created plenty of shoddy articles that have gone unpublished and teen trips that have failed to meet minimum enrollment. But Fake Grimlock's message reminds me to reassess and refine my mission, values, and presentation as often as I create new products.

To create a self-directed career, build more than a product: build a personality.

23

How to Light Your Mind on Fire

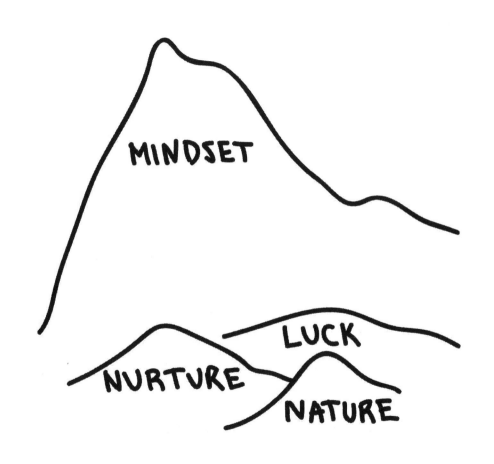

Perhaps our biggest unanswered question thus far is: How do you find the spark that helps you transition from external motivation to internal motivation?

Where did the inspiration that motivates Laura Dekker, Celina Dill, Sean Aiken, Jonah Meyer, Carsie Blanton, and the others featured in this book come from?

Or more simply: How do you light your mind on fire?

The answer lies somewhere in the intersection between nature, nurture, luck, and mindset.

Most self-directed learners are, in my nonscientific observation, blessed with a genetic predisposition for independent thought, pattern recognition, and creative problem-solving. If they choose to take on the challenges of school or college, they can handle the intellectual workload. They are, in other words, "bright." That, I believe, is the *nature* factor.

Most self-directed learners also enjoy a certain level of privilege: a combination of financial resources, parental or family support, and cultural validation that enables them to travel the world, develop a craft, hire tutors, take internships, and make other valuable, nontraditional investments in their educations. That's the *nurture* factor.

Luck is an undeniable factor in self-directed success, as well. Just as I was getting burnt out studying astrophysics in college, for example, a friend appeared wielding a book about alternative education. What if he hadn't? Would I have dropped out of school to teach snowboarding (as I briefly considered)? Would I have taken a different and ultimately less fulfilling path? The *luck* factor exists, and while we certainly create much of our own luck, the world conspires to create much of it for us, too.

But finding your spark requires a fourth and most important factor: *mindset*.

As described by the Stanford psychologist Carol Dweck, a mindset is a belief about your intelligence, talents, and personality. In Dweck's system, there are two mindsets: fixed and growth. Here's how she describes them in a nutshell.

> *People with a fixed mindset believe that their traits are just givens. They have a certain amount of brains and talent and nothing can change that. . . . So people in this mindset worry about their traits and how adequate they are. They have something to prove to themselves and others.*

> *People with a growth mindset, on the other hand, see their qualities as things that can be developed through their dedication and effort. Sure they're happy if they're brainy or talented, but that's just the starting point. They understand that no one has ever accomplished great things—not Mozart, Darwin, or Michael Jordan—without years of passionate practice and learning.*

The differences between people with fixed and growth mindsets, as Dweck has rigorously documented, are huge. Growth-oriented people do better in sports, relationships, business, parenting, formal studies, and informal lifelong learning.

Here's another way to think of mindset. If you believe that you have some control over your learning and achievements, you at least have a chance of making a positive change in your life. But if you believe that your performance is forever limited by a lack of innate gifts, general abilities, or resources, then there's no chance at all that you'll do the necessary work to improve. "Those who see the setbacks as evidence that they lack the necessary gift," the writer Geoff Colvin observes, "will give up—quite logically, in light of their beliefs."

The best thing about the *mindset* factor is that, unlike nature, nurture, or luck, mindset is largely under our control. As with a set of clothes, we can switch from a fixed mindset to a growth mindset. This switch may be difficult—it's easy to get attached to old clothes, especially when our friends are all wearing the same wardrobe—but it's entirely possible.

My switch began at Deer Crossing Camp by developing the habit of closely monitoring my internal monologue (as described in the "Cages and Keys" chapter). It continued there in 2003 when, as a first-year instructor, I almost got fired for avoiding work projects in order to read *100 Years of Solitude*. Jim (the camp director) gave me direct feedback, telling me that I either needed to change my habits or hit the road. I chose to make the change.

Having the opportunity to develop a growth mindset early in life prepared me to deal constructively with failures later in life. In 2008, for example, I applied for a job leading groups of young adults around South America as part of a gap-year program. I was extremely excited for this opportunity; I felt prepared; I had all the right credentials, and I nailed the interviews. But a few weeks later the director called and told me that I didn't get the position. There were 150 applicants for two spots, and I simply didn't make the cut.

After a few days of moping, I realized that I could either look at this as a condemnation of my abilities—the fixed mindset response—or as an excuse to learn and try something new—the growth mindset response. Choosing the latter, I e-mailed the director back and asked him if he would help me start my own international trip-leading company for teenage unschoolers. He said yes! I e-mailed a friend and asked her if she wanted to help me run my first trip, and she said yes as well. Soon I opened my first business bank account, and half a year later I was trekking around Argentina with nine teenagers on the very first Unschool Adventures trip.

This, I believe, is how we light our minds on fire. By choosing to look at failures as opportunities, challenges as adventures, and life as an infinite game, we kindle our self-motivation.

I'm not sure how Laura, Celina, Sean, Jonah, Carsie, and the other self-directed learners featured in this book developed such a powerful growth mindset, and perhaps they couldn't even answer that question themselves. It's not like turning on a bulb, after all; it's a continuous series of little decisions that add up to a much larger whole. Nature, nurture, and luck certainly played roles, but the learners themselves played an unquestionably important part as well.

Self-directed learners are regular human beings with limits, faults, and deficiencies just like everyone else—but they're people who, by conscious choice, see themselves as forever capable of learning, growing, and positively changing.

If you actively choose a growth mindset, everything is possible. If you don't, little is. Begin making this change today, and no matter your starting point, you'll embark on becoming the self-directed learner you want to be.

Stop focusing on the uncontrollable parts of your life— the nature, nurture, and luck factors—and start working hard on developing your growth mindset. That's the true art of self-directed learning.

Notes, Asides, Secrets, and Acknowledgments

Below you'll find notes about my sources, suggestions for further reading, thank-yous, and commentary that didn't make it into the chapter. It's totally worth reading!

Introduction

The summer camp I attended as a child was Deer Crossing Camp (http://www.deercrossingcamp.com) which, at the time of this writing, was entering its 32nd year of continuing operation.

The book by John Taylor Gatto that blew my mind was *A Different Kind of Teacher*.

Not Back to School Camp (http://www.nbtsc.org) was, at the time of this writing, also still operating, and I've worked there every year since 2006.

Learn more about my company, Unschool Adventures, at http://www.unschooladventures.com.

The Girl Who Sailed Around the World

Laura Dekker kindly gave me permission to share this story, e-mailing me all the way from New Zealand. You can learn more about her by googling her profile in *Outside* magazine, watching the TEDx talk she gave, and finding a copy of the feature-length documentary about her voyage, *Maidentrip*.

What Self-Directed Learners Do

Do you like that map and compass analogy? I do. Whenever I'm backpacking on a trail, I appreciate the fact someone has done the hard work of blazing a path through the wilderness for me. Without such paths, I probably would never have begun to appreciate the outdoors. But I also know that the best outdoor gems are almost always off the beaten path, and all you need to find them are a few basic backcountry navigation skills. Self-directed learning is like navigating the wilderness of "getting an education." Pretty decent analogy? Right, guys? Right?

What Self-Directed Learners Don't Do

Fellow Berkeley undergraduate Nate Singer and I created the original *Never Taught to Learn* course through the De-Cal (Democratic Education at Cal) program. We horribly over-enrolled it but managed to keep our heads on. Leading a class for 70 fellow undergrads as a 20-year-old is a hardcore challenge. The next semester I ran the course again, by myself, with a much smaller group. (Nate's also the guy who handed me the John Taylor Gatto book.)

If someone knits me a beanie like the one that I lost, it will *make my day*.

Consensual Learning

How old do you need to be to make a consensual decision about your education? That's an open question. My own work is biased towards teenagers and young adults, most of whom I believe to be fully capable (or very nearly capable) of full consent. For younger kids, obtaining consent isn't always an option, but modeling it is.

Can you learn and grow in a nonconsensual learning environment? Yes, of course. Flowers can bloom in the most inhospitable places. I don't believe, however, that this is very good excuse for coercing someone (or yourself) into a long-term education situation that feels perpetually painful and unproductive.

The quote from Ana Martin, the mom behind "The Libertarian Homeschooler" page on Facebook, was used with permission.

Autonomy, Mastery, Purpose

The idea behind the illustration is "carry your own carrot." In other words: motivate yourself. My illustrator Shona came up with that one. I love it! (Even if a "sticks and carrots" motivational system is what we're trying to avoid.)

Celina's family found the 50 different families in 17 different countries with whom they stayed through the Servas network. (Google it.) Waldorf schools hosted the dance classes that the family taught to fund their travels.

Check out photos of Celina's tiny house construction project on her blog: http://mytinyabode.blogspot.com. Celina gave me permission to share her story.

Autonomy, mastery, and purpose are the building blocks for all intrinsically motivated behavior, as proposed by the psychologists Edward Deci and Richard Ryan. To learn more, I highly recommend Deci's book *Why We Do What We Do*, along with Daniel Pink's book *Drive*, from which I originally learned about intrinsic motivation. (In Deci's and Ryan's language, the three ingredients are autonomy, mastery, and relatedness. Pink rebranded the third one as *purpose* in his book.)

I really love the meaning of the word *autotelic*. (Too bad it's such a mouthful.) Csikszentmihalyi is another author in the "positive psychology" camp—along with Deci & Ryan, Martin Seligman, Abraham Maslow, and many others—who's worth reading. The autotelic quote came from Csikszentmihalyi's 1997 book, *Finding Flow*.

Discipline, Dissected

In this chapter I combine the advice found in Stephen Pressfield's wonderful book, *The War of Art*, and Paul Graham's life-changing essay, *What You'll Wish You'd Known*. Read all of Paul Graham's essays for free on http://www.paulgraham.com.

Cages and Keys

This is the first of many chapters that owes its existence to Jim Wiltens and Deer Crossing Camp. Nowhere else (and from no one else) have I learned so much about learning how to learn.

If you happen to be young, reading this story, and planning to go to Deer Crossing Camp—I apologize for ruining the night walk surprise.

Whenever a camper says "I can't" at Deer Crossing, there are actually three things that an instructor suggests as a replacement:

- Say "T'NACI", i.e., "I can't" spelled backwards. There's a whole story about the T'NACI monster—which I won't recount for you—that's part of the camp's genius.
- Say "I choose not to": a basic acknowledgment of consent.
- Say "I could if I..."

Examining your self-talk, identifying irrational beliefs, and attempting to replace those beliefs with rational ones are the same steps behind Cognitive Behavioral Therapy.

Second Right Answers

Sean gave me permission to share this story. But I didn't ask permission to create an illustration of his awesome dreadlocks. I hope he likes it.

The "multiple right answers" idea originally came from Jim Wiltens.

Googling Everything

Austin Kleon's quote came from his incredible book, *Steal Like an Artist*, which was a huge inspiration for this book and its illustrations.

Bryan (the guy with the broken ankle) shared his story with me on the condition that I pass along the message that he traveled against the advice of doctors and doesn't necessarily recommend this approach for other people.

Perhaps the most important Internet skill is distinguishing between factual and nonfactual content online. My friend and journalist Michelle Nijhuis has a wonderful instructional article about this, entitled "The Pocket Guide to Bullshit Prevention": http://www.lastwordonnothing.com/2014/04/29/the-pocket-guide-to-bullshit-prevention/.

Check out Will Richardson's book, *Why School?: How Education Must Change When Learning and Information Are Everywhere*, for further insights on the integration of technology into education and schooling.

E-mailing Strangers

Jonah, who gave me permission to share his story, was a member of *North Star: Self-Directed Learning for Teens* in Hadley, Massachusetts, at the time that he became passionate about chemistry. If you haven't heard about North Star, check it out (http://www.northstarteens.org): it's an innovative model for supporting self-directed teens, and it's spreading.

Inspiration for the e-mail writing advice came from "How to Get a Busy Person to Respond to Your E-mail: 5 rules for good e-mail etiquette" by Mattan Griffel (https://medium.com/@mattangriffel/how-to-get-a-busy-person-to-respond-to-your-email-52e5d4d69671).

The Digital Paper Trail

Warning: *Girl Walk // All Day* contains explicit lyrics. (Sorry, I'm probably too late!)

I attempted to contact Anne Marsen to ask her permission to share this story, but I was unsuccessful. My primary source for the story was the *New York Times* article about her and *Girl Walk // All Day*: http://www.nytimes.com/2011/03/06/magazine/06GirlWalk-t.html.

I wrote more extensively about creating shareable online content ("deliverables") in my second book, *Better Than College* (http://www.better-than-college.com).

Information Versus Knowledge

My editor told me that I gave MOOCs a bad wrap in this chapter. I agreed with her defense of the dropout rate: on the Internet, where something is free, the dropout rate will naturally be huge because there's no disincentive. But I hold fast to my original instinct regarding MOOCs. I think they're a great idea for scaling schooling from a business perspective, but they're not innovative when it comes to departing from the lecture model.

The 95% MOOC dropout rate is documented here: http://www.businessweek.com/news/2014-01-21/harvard-online-courses-dropped-by-95-percent-of-registered-study-says.

Alone, Together

The idea for the Unschool Adventures Writing Retreat came from National Novel-Writing Month (NaNoWriMo), a challenge to write 50,000 words in the calendar month of November. Launched in 1999 by freelance writer Chris Baty, NaNoWriMo encourages budding novelists to turn off their inner editors and focus instead on daily word output. I tried and failed twice to meet a NaNoWriMo goal. The first time I got to 11,000 words, the second time around 30,000. More: http://nanowrimo.org.

If you're a solo entrepreneur, freelancer, or part of a very small business team, I highly recommend you check out your closest "co-working" center: a place to work in an open office atmosphere alongside others with similar careers. (I wrote big chunks of this book at my own local center which offered much-needed ping-pong and conversation breaks.)

The comment by Michael F. Booth (username: mechanical_fish) can be found here: https://news.ycombinator.com/item?id=2462777.

Nerd Clans

Inspiration from this chapter came from Paul Graham's essay, *Why Nerds are Unpopular*.

Living and working in the student co-ops was the most important part of my college experience. If you have the chance to join one, I highly recommend it. Do an online search for "student co-op [your area]" to find both formal co-ops (i.e., those associated with large organizations like the Berkeley Student Co-ops) and informal ones created by people who are simply passionate about cooperative group living.

Learning How to Learn

Here's where my inspiration for some of the leadership retreat activities came from:

- Entrepreneur weekend: Tina Seelig of the Stanford Design School
- Paperclip weekend: Kyle MacDonald's One Red Paperclip project: http://youtu.be/BE8b02EdZvw
- Hobo weekend: The Deer Crossing Camp ascent trip

Here's the source of the Seth Godin quote: http://sethgodin. typepad.com/seths_blog/2013/09/the-truth-about-the-war-for-talent.html.

"People get hired for professional skills and fired for personal skills" came from Pieter Spinder of the Knowmads Business School in Amsterdam.

The Dance Lesson

Grace Llewellyn (author of *The Teenage Liberation Handbook* and founder/director of Not Back to School Camp) originally connected me to Alicia Pons. Thanks, Gracey.

Alicia's sayings were drawn from my fuzzy memory; they're not direct quotes.

Indescribable Sexiness

I adapted this workshop from Jim Wiltens, who teaches these techniques as part of the Deer Crossing Camp instructor training. I altered the phrasing and acronyms; Jim's original terminology is PEGSS (Posture, Eyes, Gestures, Sound, Smile) and RIQE (Reflective listening, I-messages, open-ended Questions, and Experience).

I chose the acronym PASHE because the word "pash" is a fun colloquial word from the early 1900s that describes either a short, passionate fling or a sloppy French kiss.

I really do love online cat videos.

Deliberate Practice

Information about Ericsson's research is widely available online; my primary source was the excellent book *Talent is Overrated* by Geoff Colvin.

Daniel Coyle's advice was adapted from his helpful manual for putting deliberate practice into action: *The Little Book of Talent*.

Pumping Poop for the Win

Let me share a secret with you: I'm working hard on starting my camp / (un)school / big program *right now*. I'm super excited for it. Hopefully, by the time you read this, I'll have more details to share with you. Stay tuned on my blog (http://blakeboles.com) or by stalking me on Facebook (http://www.facebook.com/blakeboles).

Jim Wiltens generously shared his time with me over the course of multiple years, as I bugged him repeatedly for the details of his fascinating life. He also graciously accepted the fact that I used the word *poop* in the chapter title.

Passion, Skill, Market

Carsie Blanton gave me permission to share her story in the midst of preparing for her Kickstarter-fueled musical tour of the United States. If you get the chance to see her perform, don't miss it: http://www.carsieblanton.com.

Find more of Tina Seelig's career advice by googling her Stanford eCorner video on "interests, skills, and market" or reading her book, *What I Wish I Knew When I Was 20*.

The passion / skill / market approach doesn't account for the "moonlighting" approach of making money with a day job (which you're not passionate about) and working on hobbies at other times. Can you take this approach and still be a self-directed learner? As long as you're consciously aware of your approach and you keep a close eye on your sanity levels, then yes, I think it's possible. (Personally, I'd rather risk impoverishment in the pursuit of a passion / skill / market overlap.)

Time Wealth

Dev Carey, who works with me at Unschool Adventures and recently launched his own gap-year program (see: http://www.hdcss.org), authorized this story.

Career Advice from a Robot Dinosaur

Read more @FAKEGRIMLOCK on Twitter (https://twitter.com/FAKEGRIMLOCK) and http://fakegrimlock.com.

The out-of-persona interview with the mind behind the scenes can be found here: http://thenextweb.com/insider/2012/03/31/breakfast-of-champions-meet-the-man-known-as-fakegrimlock/.

The post about personality, entitled "Minimum Viable Personality," is here: http://avc.com/2011/09/minimum-viable-personality/.

How to Light Your Mind on Fire

Read more about Carol Dweck's theory in her book, *Mindset*, or online at her website, http://www.mindsetonline.com (from which the quotes are taken).

The Geoff Colvin quote is from his book *Talent is Overrated*.

Final Acknowledgments

This book wouldn't have been possible without the generous support of 264 Kickstarter backers (https://www.kickstarter.com/projects/blakeboles/the-art-of-self-directed-learning), the members of my book superhero team, the self-directed learners who shared their stories with me, and Franki Wangen. Thanks, everyone.

Many important people helped transform my manuscript into a well-polished and independently published final product. Lori Mortimer (editor) carved my manuscript up like a Thanksgiving turkey and then helped me sew it back together again; Shona Warwick-Smith (illustrator) "got" my message and independently devised many of the illustrations; Ashley Halsey combined words and graphics into a beautiful PDF; and Dawn Forbes proofread like a boss.

About the Author

Blake Boles builds exciting alternatives to traditional school for self-directed young people. He directs the company Unschool Adventures and is the author of *Better Than College* and *College Without High School*. Blake and his work have appeared on TEDx, The Huffington Post, USA Today, The New York Times, BBC Travel, Fox Business, Ignite, NPR affiliate radio, and the blogs of The Wall Street Journal and Wired.com.

To stay in the loop regarding Blake's projects and writings, join his author mailing list: http://blakeboles.com/list/.

Connect with him directly at yourstruly@blakeboles.com.

28635972R00126

Made in the USA
San Bernardino, CA
03 January 2016